MW00955101

DAVE SIM
Creator, Writer,
Pencil & Ink Interior Art
& Cover Painting

LOU COPELAND
Digital Production,
Research Assistance

SANDEEP ATWAL
Scans

www.judenhass.com

PRODUCED BY
AARDVARK-VANAHEIM INC.
P.O. BOX 1674, STATION C
KITCHENER, ON N2G 4R2

ALL RIGHTS TO THIS WORK
HAVE BEEN DONATED TO
THE PUBLIC DOMAIN BY
ITS AUTHOR, DAVE SIM,
EFFECTIVE NOV. 7, 2014.

THE SIXTIETH ANNIVERSARY OF THE LIBERATION OF AUSCHWITZ IN 2005 MADE ME THINK THAT EVERY CREATIVE PERSON SHOULD CONSIDER DOING A WORK ADDRESSING THE SHOAH — THE PREFERRED JUDAIC TERM FOR THE HOLOCAUST — AT SOME POINT IN HIS OR HER LIFE

AND IT SEEMS TO ME THAT THIS IS NOWHERE TRUER THAN HERE IN THE COMIC-BOOK FIELD WHICH WAS CREATED, DEVELOPED AND BUILT PRIMARILY BY JEWS, PAINSTAKINGLY, ONE COMIC BOOK AT A TIME, BEGINNING IN THE 1930'S WHEN JEW HATRED WAS ABOUT TO MANIFEST ITSELF IN ONE OF THE GREATEST — IF NOT THE GREATEST — ATROCITIES EVER COMMITTED BY MAN AGAINST MANKIND.

TO SEE THE ROUGH-HEWN BARRACKS AT AUSCHWITZ FILLED WITH ORDINARY MEN WHO HAD BEEN ABUSED, BEATEN AND MALTREATED, STARVED UNTIL THEY HAD WASTED AWAY TO VIRTUAL HUMAN SKELETONS IT IS WORTH REMEMBERING THAT, BUT FOR GEOGRAPHIC HAPPENSTANCE AND THE GRACE OF GOD, ANY ONE OF THOSE ORDINARY MEN COULD HAVE JUST AS EASILY BEEN...

BECAUSE THE ONLY "CRIME" FOR WHICH THESE MEN WHOM YOU SEE HERE — AND MILLIONS OF OTHER MEN AND WOMEN AND CHILDREN — HAD BEEN "CONVICTED" AND FOR WHICH THEY WERE BEING "PUNISHED" IN THE BARRACKS AT AUSCHWITZ, AT BERGEN BELSEN, AT BUCHENWALD AND THE OTHER CAMPS WAS THAT, LIKE THESE FAMOUS COMIC-BOOK CREATORS, THEY HAD BEEN BORN JEWISH.

"LEST WE FORGET"... "NEVER AGAIN"...ARE FINE AND NOBLE-SOUNDING SENTIMENTS WHICH HAVE ATTACHED THEMSELVES TO THE HISTORICAL REMEMBRANCE OF WHAT WAS DONE TO THESE INNOCENT INDIVIDUALS AND MILLIONS OF OTHERS LIKE THEM.

BUT IT SEEMS TO ME THAT THE WORDS ARE LARGELY MEANINGLESS IF (AS HAS BEEN THE CASE TO NOW) IN MOVIES, IN BOOKS, IN PLAYS AND IN DOCUMENTS OF THE HISTORICAL RECORD THEY ARE EXPRESSIONS LARGELY IF NOT EXCLUSIVELY BEING ENUNCIATED BY JEWS. IF THERE IS A CHANCE OF SYSTEMIC JEW HATRED BEING ELIMINATED FROM OUR SOCIETY, IT CAN'T JUST BE JEWS WHO SPEAK OUT AGAINST IT.

THE SHOAH WAS DONE TO JEWS — AND, YES, TO OTHERS AS WELL. BUT THE FACT THAT "TO OTHERS AS WELL" HAS BECOME A UNIVERSAL INTERJECTION WHEN THE SUBJECT OF THE HOLOCAUST COMES UP, IT SEEMS TO ME, POINTS TO A CENTRAL AND MALIGNANT EVASIVENESS ON THE PART OF NON-JEWS.

THE SHOAH WAS DONE TO JEWS, SO OF COURSE JEWS ARE GOING TO REMEMBER IT, CONTEMPLATE IT, DOCUMENT IT, AND FOR JEWS "LEST WE FORGET" AND "NEVER AGAIN" ARE NATURALLY A CORE PART OF THEIR POST-1945 CULTURAL IDENTITY WITH THEIR CONTINUED EXISTENCE AS A PEOPLE IMPLICITLY VERY MUCH AT RISK AND VERY MUCH IN DOUBT.

JEWISH REMEMBRANCE OF THE SHOAH, DISTILLED TO ITS ESSENCE OF "NEVER AGAIN" IMPLIES THE SELF-PRESERVATION OF THE LIFE OF NOT ONLY EACH INDIVIDUAL JEW WHEREVER HE OR SHE LIVES, BUT OF ALL OF GOD'S CHOSEN PEOPLE WHEREVER THEIR COLLECTIVE CONTINUED EXISTENCE IS THREATENED — AS THAT COLLECTIVE CONTINUED EXISTENCE OF THE EUROPEAN JEW WAS VERY MUCH THREATENED IN EUROPE IN THE 1930'S AND 1940'S.

AND IS, TO ME, SIGNIFICANTLY DIFFERENT FROM NON-JEWS SAYING "NEVER AGAIN" FROM BEHIND THE SHELTERING AND DISINGENUOUS FAÇADE OF:

"HOW COULD THIS HAVE HAPPENED?"

IMPLYING AS IT DOES THAT THE SHOAH HAD BEEN A GENUINELY UNTHINKABLE ACT WITHOUT PRECEDENT IN NON-JEWISH SOCIETY...AS IF THE SHOAH HAD BEEN A ONE-IN-A-MILLION HAPPENSTANCE WHICH COULD ONLY HAVE HAPPENED IN GERMANY AND ONLY UNDER THE NAZI REGIME, WHEREAS I BELIEVE THE HISTORICAL RECORD OF NON-JEWISH CULTURE AND ITS TOLERANCE FOR AND EMBRACING OF JEW HATRED SHOWS, INSTEAD, THAT THE SHOAH WAS VERY MUCH...

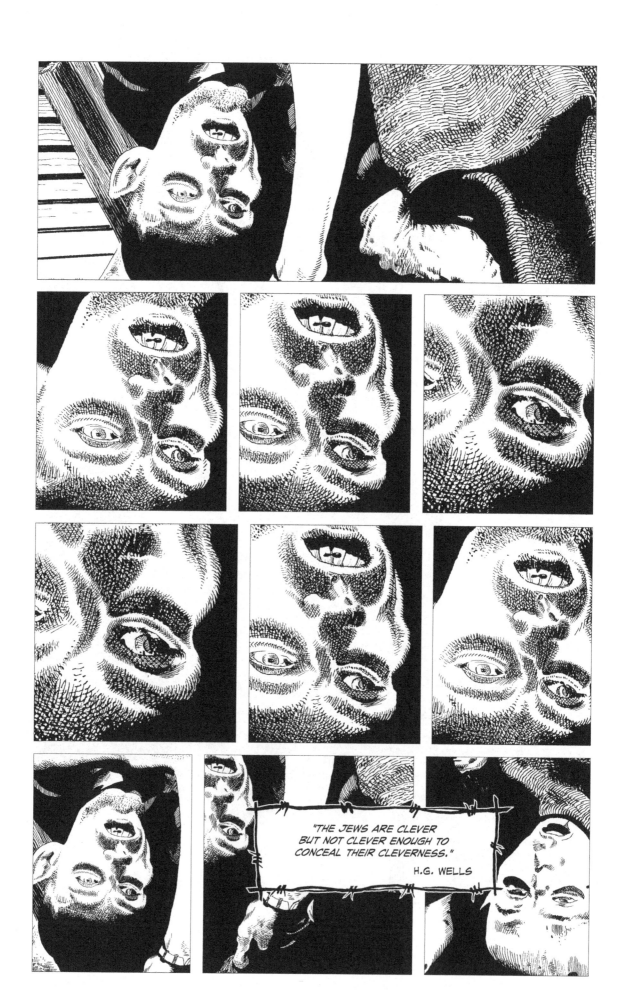

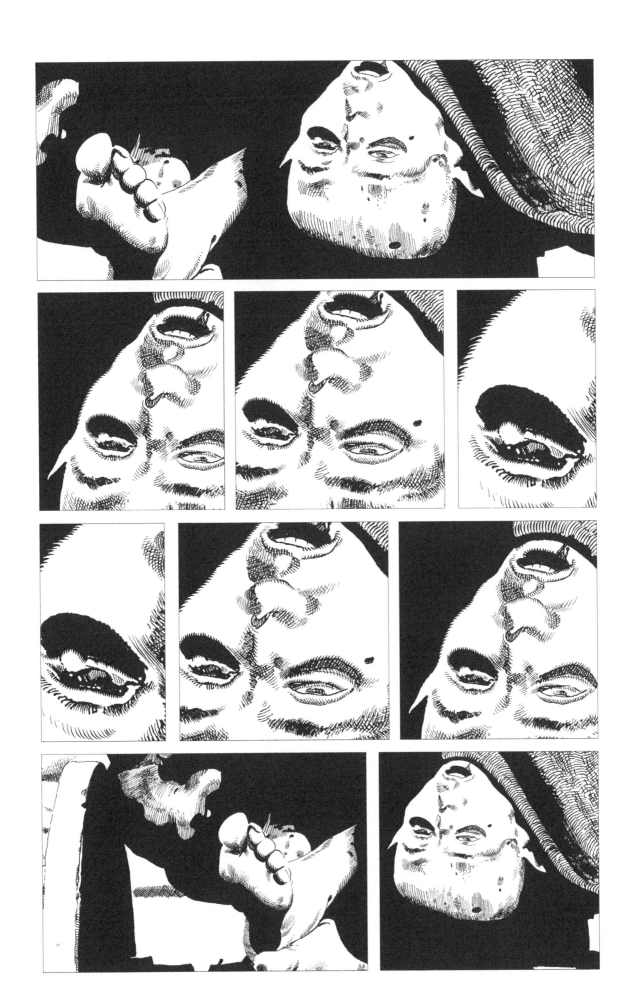

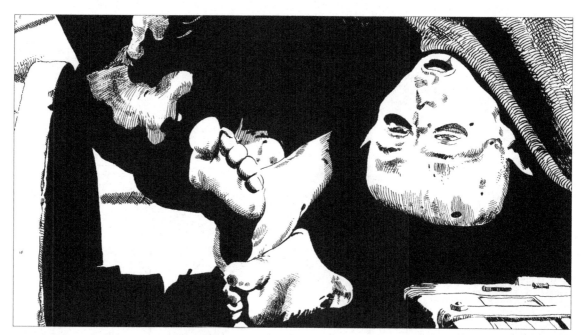

DIE ENDLÖSUNG [GERMAN: THE FINAL SOLUTION]

CHUB'N [HEBREW: DESTRUCTION]

SHO'AH [HEBREW: CATASTROPHE]

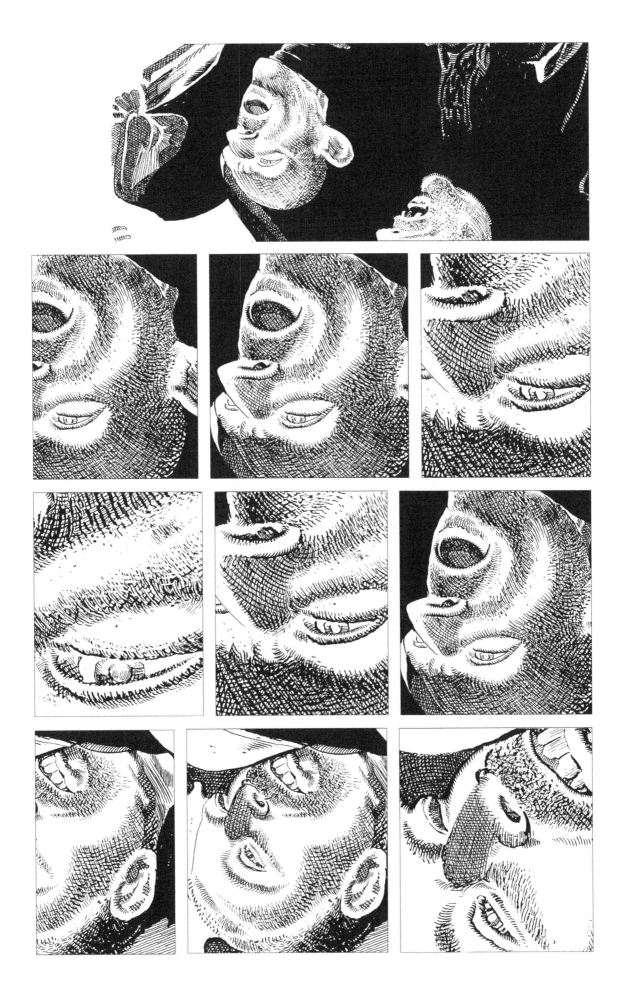

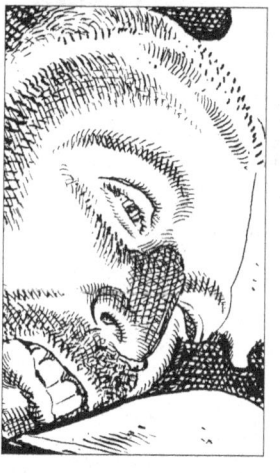

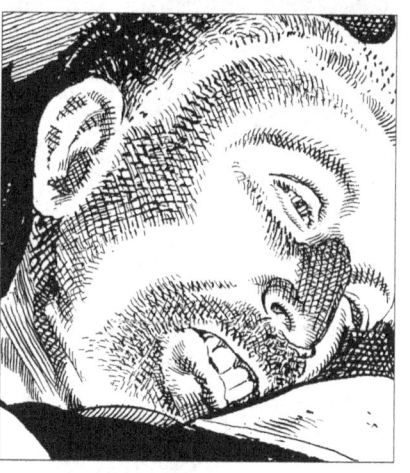

"OUR LICE ARE ON OUR HEADS
BUT THE JEW'S ARE IN HIS HEART."
RUSSIAN PROVERB

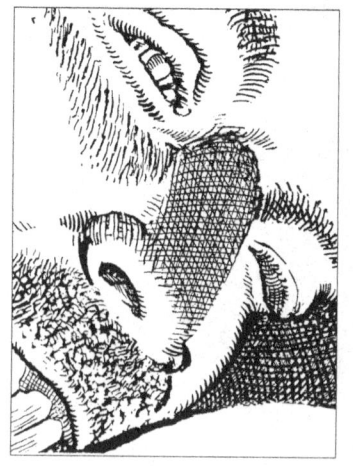
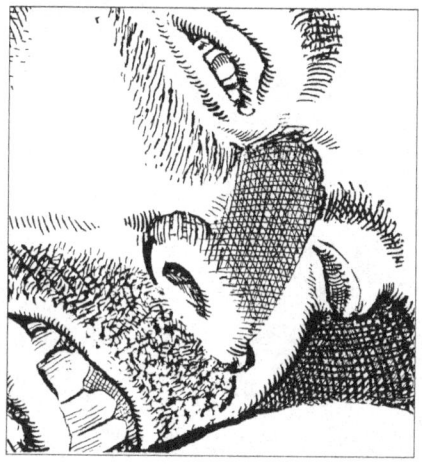
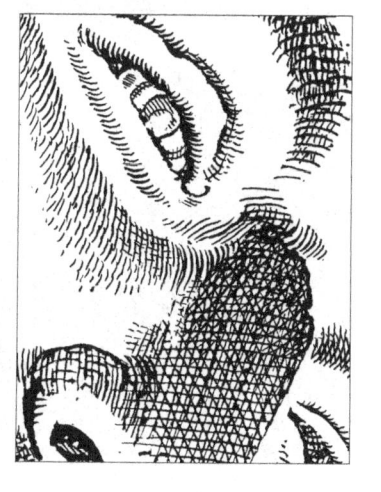

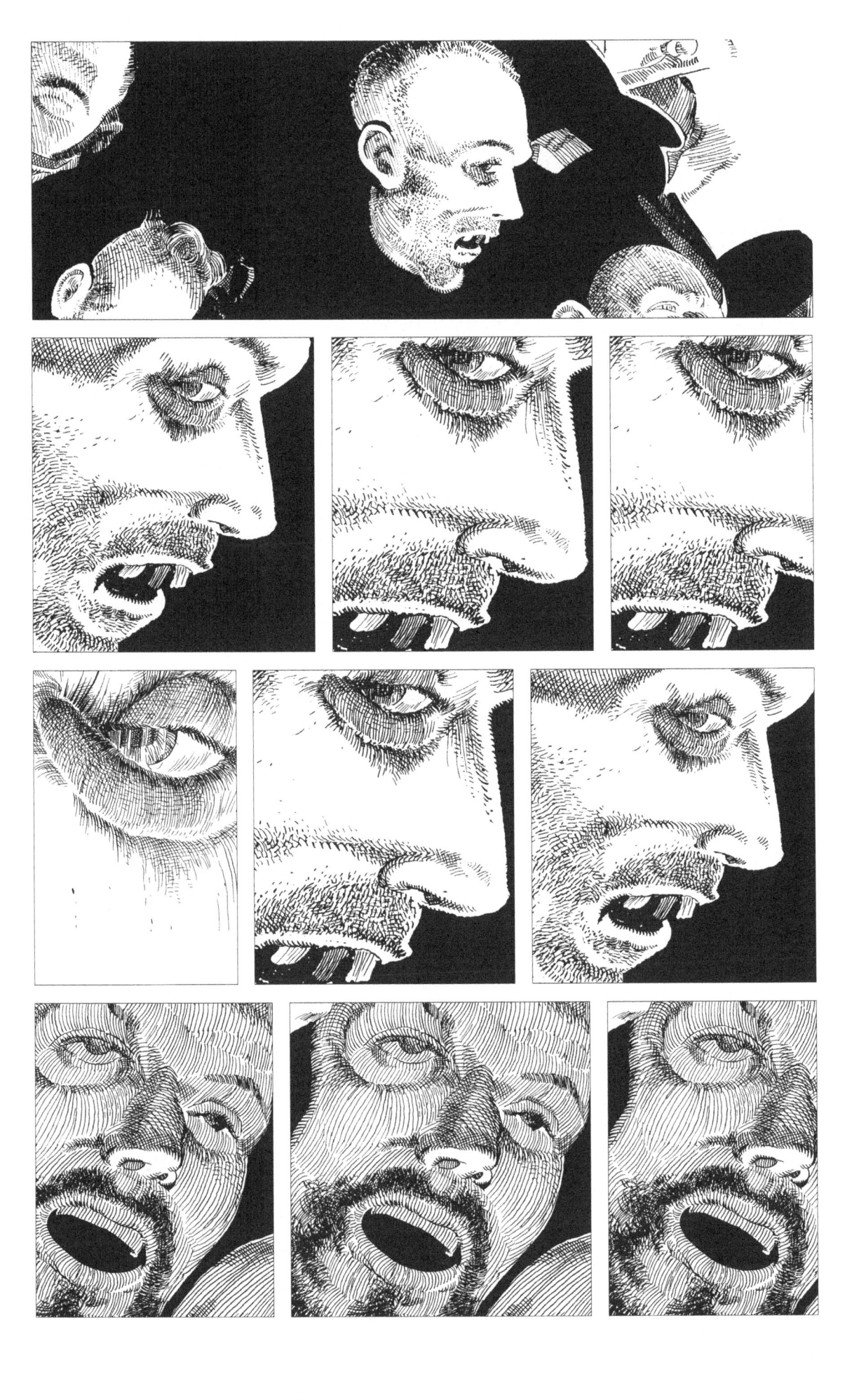

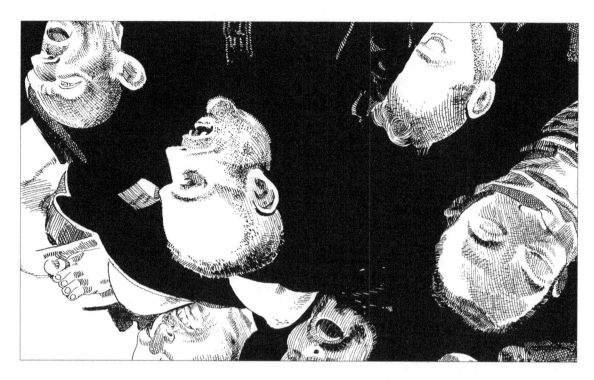

UNTERMENSCHEN [GERMAN:
SUBHUMANS]

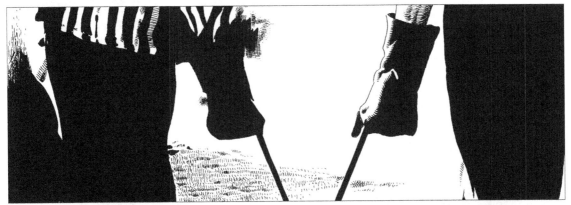

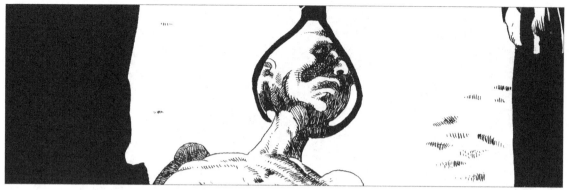

JUDENREIN [GERMAN: CLEANSED OF JEWS]

PORRAJAMOS [SINTI AND ROMA: THE GREAT DEVOURING]

HOLOKAUSTOS [A GREEK TERM FROM THE SEPTUAGINT TRANSLATING THE HEBREW TERM *OLAH* MEANING *"A COMPLETELY CONSUMED BURNT OFFERING"*]

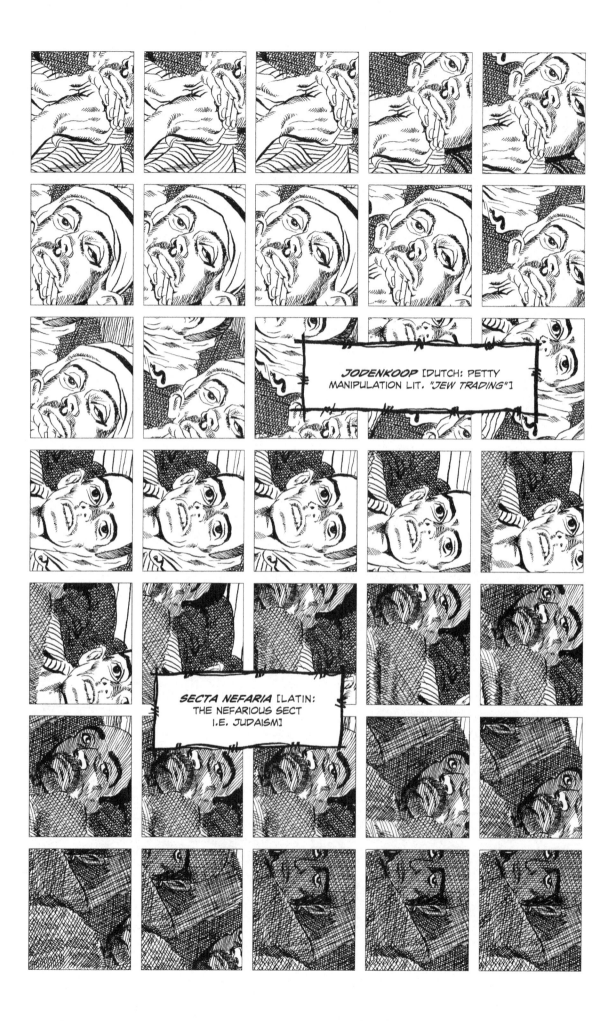

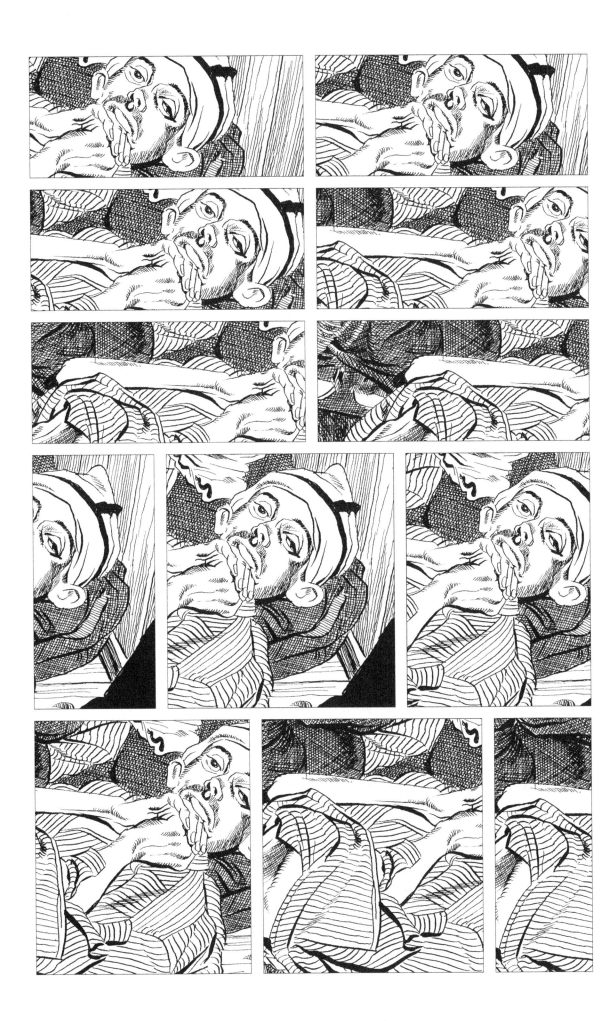

"JUDGMENT DAY SHALL NOT COME UNTIL THE MUSLIM FIGHTS THE JEW, WHERE THE JEW WILL HIDE BEHIND TREES AND STONES AND THE TREE AND THE STONE WILL SPEAK AND SAY 'MUSLIM, BEHIND ME IS A JEW. COME AND KILL HIM.'"

THE HADITH
(SAYINGS OF THE
PROPHET MUHAMMAD)

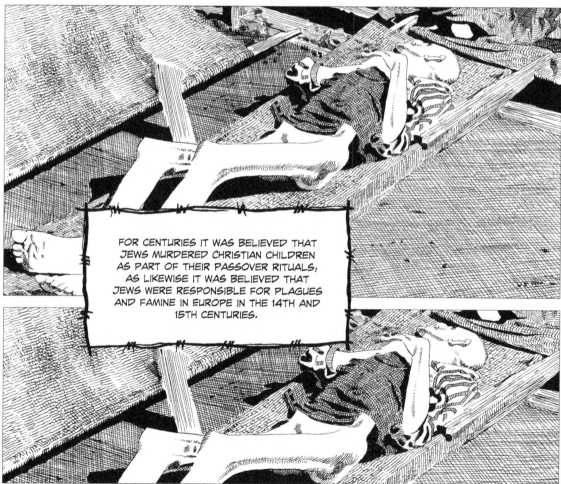

FOR CENTURIES IT WAS BELIEVED THAT
JEWS MURDERED CHRISTIAN CHILDREN
AS PART OF THEIR PASSOVER RITUALS,
AS LIKEWISE IT WAS BELIEVED THAT
JEWS WERE RESPONSIBLE FOR PLAGUES
AND FAMINE IN EUROPE IN THE 14TH AND
15TH CENTURIES.

"THE HEBREWS HAVE EVER BEEN VAGRANTS, OR ROBBERS OR SLAVES, OR SEDITIOUS. THEY ARE STILL VAGABONDS UPON THE EARTH, AND ABHORRED BY MEN, YET AFFIRMING THAT HEAVEN AND EARTH AND ALL MANKIND WERE CREATED FOR THEM ALONE."

VOLTAIRE (18TH CENTURY PHILOSOPHER)
PHILOSOPHICAL DICTIONARY
1764

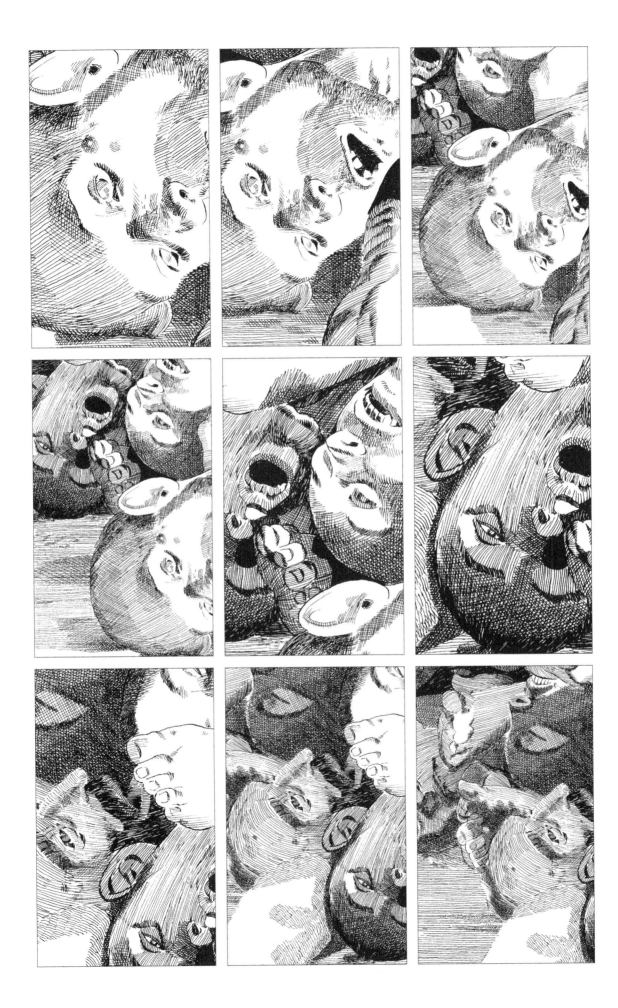

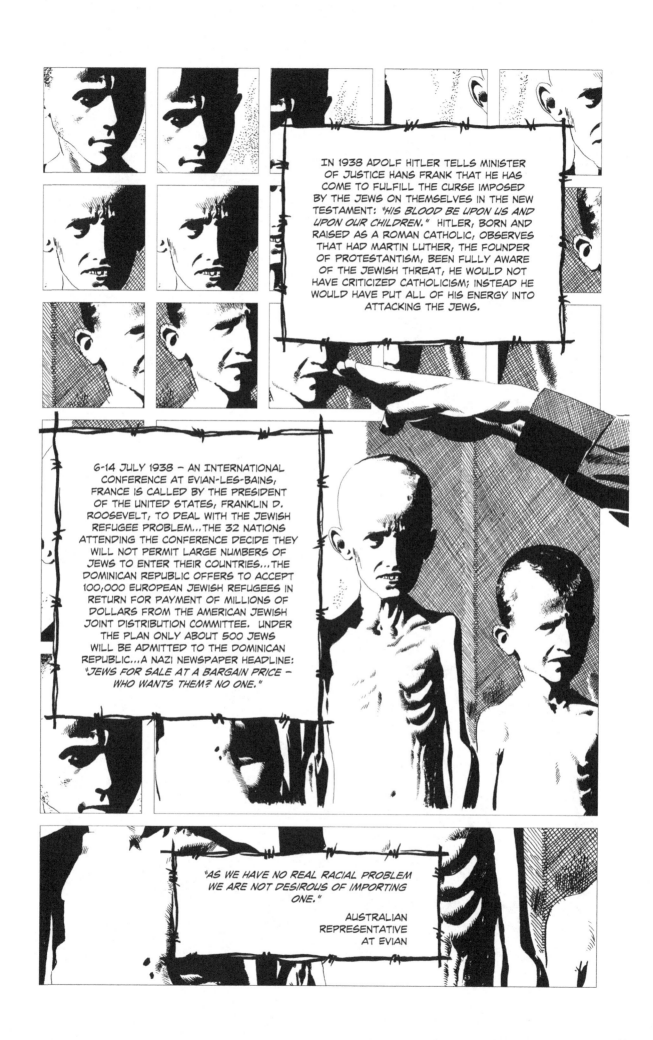

IN 1938 ADOLF HITLER TELLS MINISTER OF JUSTICE HANS FRANK THAT HE HAS COME TO FULFILL THE CURSE IMPOSED BY THE JEWS ON THEMSELVES IN THE NEW TESTAMENT: *"HIS BLOOD BE UPON US AND UPON OUR CHILDREN."* HITLER, BORN AND RAISED AS A ROMAN CATHOLIC, OBSERVES THAT HAD MARTIN LUTHER, THE FOUNDER OF PROTESTANTISM, BEEN FULLY AWARE OF THE JEWISH THREAT, HE WOULD NOT HAVE CRITICIZED CATHOLICISM; INSTEAD HE WOULD HAVE PUT ALL OF HIS ENERGY INTO ATTACKING THE JEWS.

6-14 JULY 1938 — AN INTERNATIONAL CONFERENCE AT EVIAN-LES-BAINS, FRANCE IS CALLED BY THE PRESIDENT OF THE UNITED STATES, FRANKLIN D. ROOSEVELT, TO DEAL WITH THE JEWISH REFUGEE PROBLEM...THE 32 NATIONS ATTENDING THE CONFERENCE DECIDE THEY WILL NOT PERMIT LARGE NUMBERS OF JEWS TO ENTER THEIR COUNTRIES...THE DOMINICAN REPUBLIC OFFERS TO ACCEPT 100,000 EUROPEAN JEWISH REFUGEES IN RETURN FOR PAYMENT OF MILLIONS OF DOLLARS FROM THE AMERICAN JEWISH JOINT DISTRIBUTION COMMITTEE. UNDER THE PLAN ONLY ABOUT 500 JEWS WILL BE ADMITTED TO THE DOMINICAN REPUBLIC...A NAZI NEWSPAPER HEADLINE: *"JEWS FOR SALE AT A BARGAIN PRICE — WHO WANTS THEM? NO ONE."*

"AS WE HAVE NO REAL RACIAL PROBLEM WE ARE NOT DESIROUS OF IMPORTING ONE."

AUSTRALIAN REPRESENTATIVE AT EVIAN

A 1939 ELMO ROPER POLL CLAIMS THAT 53 PERCENT OF AMERICANS FEEL JEWS ARE *"DIFFERENT"* AND REQUIRE *"SOCIAL AND ECONOMIC RESTRICTIONS."* A GALLUP POLL THE SAME YEAR REPORTS THAT 83 PERCENT OF AMERICANS OPPOSE THE ADMISSION OF A LARGER NUMBER OF JEWISH REFUGEES.

"EDDIE AND I WERE NEVER AT THE TRUMAN HOUSE. WE WENT MAYBE TWO OR THREE TIMES ON PICNICS AND ON THE FOURTH OF JULY; BUT THE TRUMANS NEVER HAD US AT THEIR HOME. THE WALLACES [HARRY TRUMAN'S IN-LAWS] WERE ARISTOCRACY IN THESE PARTS, AND UNDER THE CIRCUMSTANCES THE TRUMANS COULDN'T AFFORD TO HAVE JEWS AT THEIR HOUSE."

BLUMA JACOBSON, WIFE OF EDDIE JACOBSON, HARRY TRUMAN'S PARTNER IN THEIR FAILED HABERDASHERY BUSINESS PRIOR TO TRUMAN ENTERING POLITICS

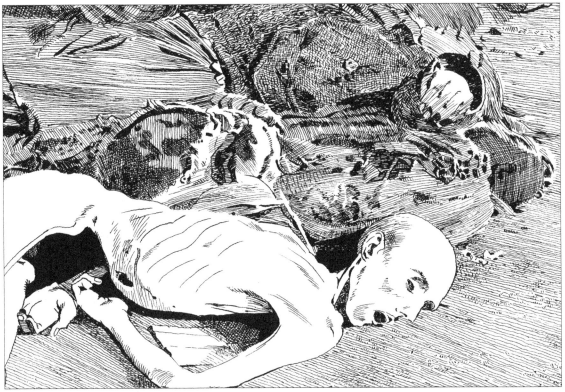

9 FEBRUARY 1939 – ANTI-JEWISH LEGISLATION IS PASSED IN ITALY.

10 FEBRUARY 1939 – POPE PIUS XI DIES. HIS UNPUBLISHED ENCYCLICAL ON RACISM AND ANTI-SEMITISM DOES NOT GO BEYOND THE VATICAN'S TRADITIONAL POLICY CONCERNING THE JEWS. THE POLICY IS BASED ON THE DOCTRINE OF ST. AUGUSTINE THAT THE JEWS ARE CAINS WHO MUST NOT BE KILLED BUT WHO MUST WANDER IN SUFFERING FOR ALL ETERNITY UNTIL THEY SEE THE LIGHT AND CHOOSE CONVERSION TO ROMAN CATHOLICISM.

"BECAUSE THE HATRED OF JEWS HAD BEEN MADE HOLY, IT BECAME LETHAL."

JAMES CARROLL
CONSTANTINE'S SWORD

MAY 1939 – IN HUNGARY, DISCRIMINATING LAWS ARE PASSED AGAINST JEWS ENGAGED IN LAW AND MEDICINE. JEWISH PARTICIPATION IN THE ECONOMY IS RESTRICTED TO SIX PERCENT.

THE MACDONALD WHITE PAPER OF 17 MAY 1939 LIMITED JEWISH IMMIGRATION TO PALESTINE TO 10,000 PEOPLE A YEAR FOR FIVE YEARS. BRITISH GOVERNMENT POLICY KEPT THE ACTUAL NUMBERS OF JEWISH IMMIGRANTS FAR BELOW THE QUOTAS SET FOR PALESTINE.

2 JUNE 1939 – THE BOSTON-BASED NEWSPAPER OF THE CHRISTIAN SCIENCE CHURCH ATTACKS JEWISH REFUGEES AS "CAUSING THEIR OWN TROUBLES."

"NO DOUBT JEWS AREN'T A LOVABLE PEOPLE – I DON'T CARE ABOUT THEM MYSELF. BUT THAT IS NOT SUFFICIENT TO EXPLAIN THE POGROM."

BRITISH PRIME MINISTER NEVILLE CHAMBERLAIN 30 JULY 1939

ASKED FOR HER OPINION ON THE WAGNER-ROGERS BILL OF 1939, LAURA DELANO, THE PRESIDENT'S COUSIN, REPLIES, "THE ONLY PROBLEM IS THAT 20,000 UGLY [JEWISH] CHILDREN WOULD ALL TOO SOON GROW UP INTO 20,000 UGLY ADULTS."

A POLITICAL ALLY OF PRESIDENT ROOSEVELT, ASSISTANT SECRETARY OF STATE BRECKINRIDGE LONG, OPPOSES "EXCESSIVE HUMANITARIANISM IN REGARDS TO THE JEWS" AND IS ENTRUSTED BY THE PRESIDENT WITH DECIDING THE QUESTION OF JEWISH IMMIGRATION TO THE U.S.

LESLIE HORE-BELISHA, GREAT BRITAIN'S SECRETARY OF STATE FOR WAR, AND A JEW, RESIGNS, LARGELY BECAUSE OF THE ANTI-JEWISH FEELINGS AMONG MEMBERS OF THE BRITISH GOVERNMENT. FOREIGN SECRETARY LORD HALIFAX AND UNDER-SECRETARY OF THE FOREIGN OFFICE ALEXANDER CADOGAN NOTE THAT HORE-BELISHA'S JEWISHNESS RENDERED HIM UNSUITABLE AS MINISTER OF INFORMATION, STATING "JEW CONTROL OF OUR PROPAGANDA WOULD BE [A] MAJOR DISASTER."

"IN FIGHTING OFF THE JEW, I AM FIGHTING THE LORD'S WORK."

ADOLF HITLER

"WE LOVE ADOLF HITLER BECAUSE WE BELIEVE – WITH A FAITH THAT IS DEEP AND UNSHAKABLE – THAT HE WAS SENT TO US BY GOD TO SAVE GERMANY."

GENERALFELD-MARSCHALL HERMANN GÖRING

IN 1940, CANADA IS A COUNTRY HOSTILE TO JEWISH IMMIGRATION. WHILE FARMERS WERE WELCOMED, THOSE OF MOST OTHER OCCUPATIONS WERE NOT. SCHOLARS AND TEACHERS, NO MATTER HOW ESTEEMED IN THEIR HOMELAND, FOUND CANADA'S UNIVERSITIES UNWILLING TO OFFER THEM POSTS. THE CANADIAN GOVERNMENT'S POSITION WAS SUMMED UP AS "NONE IS TOO MANY."

30 JANUARY 1940 – THE BRITISH EMBASSY IN BUCHAREST PRESSURES THE ROMANIAN GOVERNMENT TO PREVENT ITS SHIPS FROM CARRYING JEWISH REFUGEES.

10 MAY 1940 – POET AND ESSAYIST T.S. ELIOT WRITES THAT THE JEWS ARE THE MODERN WORLD'S FOREMOST "FORCES OF EVIL." HE CLAIMS THEY HAVE MADE THE MODERN WORLD VILE.

26 JUNE 1940 – UNITED STATES ASSISTANT SECRETARY OF STATE BRECKINRIDGE LONG DETERMINES TO OBSTRUCT THE GRANTING OF VISAS TO JEWS SEEKING ENTRY INTO THE UNITED STATES. HE SEEKS INDEFINITELY TO "DELAY AND EFFECTIVELY STOP" SUCH IMMIGRATION BY ORDERING AMERICAN CONSULS "TO PUT EVERY OBSTACLE IN THE WAY [TO] POSTPONE AND POSTPONE AND POSTPONE THE GRANTING OF VISAS." HIS GOAL WILL BE REALIZED OVER THE NEXT FOUR YEARS.

23 MAY 1940 – FRUSTRATED BY "ILLEGAL" IMMIGRATION INTO PALESTINE, BRITISH HIGH COMMISSIONER FOR PALESTINE SIR HAROLD MACMICHAEL INSISTS THAT HUNGARY ACCEPT THE RETURN OF TWO JEWS WHO HAD LEFT HUNGARY AND SETTLED IN PALESTINE IN 1934 ON TOURIST VISAS. THE HUNGARIAN GOVERNMENT REPLIES THAT THERE ARE AN "EXCESSIVE" NUMBER OF JEWS IN THEIR COUNTRY AND THE GOVERNMENT'S AIM IS THAT "AS MANY AS POSSIBLE SHOULD BE ENCOURAGED TO EMIGRATE."

15 AUGUST 1940 – ADOLF EICHMANN PROPOSES TURNING THE ISLAND OF MADAGASCAR INTO A HUGE JEWISH GHETTO WHERE JEWS WILL DIE OUT.

11 SEPTEMBER 1940 – THE JEWISH REFUGEE SHIP *QUANZA* STOPS TO REFUEL AT NORFOLK, VIRGINIA, AFTER HAVING BEEN DENIED ENTRY TO THE UNITED STATES AT NEW YORK AND TO MEXICO AT VERA CRUZ. ONE PASSENGER, A GERMAN JEW, IS RETURNED TO THE SHIP BY U.S. ARMY GUARDS AFTER LEAPING OVERBOARD NEAR THE SHORE OF HAMPTON ROADS, VIRGINIA.

26 NOVEMBER 1940 – BRITISH SECRETARY OF STATE FOR THE COLONIES, LORD LLOYD CALLS THOSE WHO ARE WORKING TO SAVE JEWISH LIVES BY ILLEGALLY TRANSPORTING THEM TO PALESTINE *"FOUL PEOPLE WHO HAD TO BE STAMPED OUT."*

12 DECEMBER 1940 – *THE SALVADOR*, A SHIP THAT SET OUT FROM VARNA, BULGARIA A MONTH BEFORE, SINKS IN THE SEA OF MARMORA. 200 JEWISH REFUGEES, INCLUDING 70 CHILDREN, DROWN. T.M. SNOW, HEAD OF THE BRITISH FOREIGN OFFICE'S REFUGEE SECTION, NOTES THAT *"THERE COULD HAVE BEEN NO MORE OPPORTUNE DISASTER FROM THE POINT OF VIEW OF STOPPING THIS [JEWISH REFUGEE] TRAFFIC [TO PALESTINE]."*

"WE WERE FORCED TO COME TO THE GRIM DECISION THAT THIS PEOPLE MUST BE MADE TO DISAPPEAR FROM THE FACE OF THE EARTH...WE HAVE TACKLED [THE ASSIGNMENT] AND CARRIED IT THROUGH WITHOUT OUR MEN AND OUR LEADERS SUFFERING ANY DAMAGE IN THEIR MINDS AND SOULS."

HEINRICH HIMMLER

"A FORTNIGHT AFTER MY ARRIVAL, I ALREADY HAD THE PRESCRIBED HUNGER, THAT CHRONIC HUNGER UNKNOWN TO FREE MEN, WHICH MAKES ONE DREAM AT NIGHT, AND SETTLES IN ALL THE LIMBS OF ONE'S BODY...ON THE BACK OF MY FEET I ALREADY HAD THOSE NUMB SORES THAT WILL NOT HEAL. I PUSH WAGONS, I WORK WITH A SHOVEL; I TURN ROTTEN IN THE RAIN; I SHIVER IN THE WIND; ALREADY MY BODY IS NO LONGER MINE: MY BELLY IS SWOLLEN, MY LIMBS EMACIATED, MY FACE IS THICK IN THE MORNING, HOLLOW IN THE EVENING; SOME OF US HAVE YELLOW SKIN, OTHERS GREY. WHEN WE DO NOT MEET EACH OTHER FOR A FEW DAYS, WE HARDLY RECOGNIZE EACH OTHER."

A CAMP SURVIVOR

"THE BEGINNING, THE END: ALL THE WORLD'S ROADS, ALL THE OUTCRIES OF MANKIND LEAD TO THIS ACCURSED PLACE. HERE IS THE KINGDOM OF NIGHT, WHERE GOD'S FACE IS HIDDEN AND A FLAMING SKY BECOMES A GRAVEYARD FOR A VANISHED PEOPLE."

ELIE WIESEL ON AUSCHWITZ-BIRKENAU

CREMATORIUM IV AT AUSCHWITZ-BIRKENAU COULD BURN ALMOST 1500 BODIES A DAY.

"WHEN JEWISH BLOOD SPURTS FROM THE KNIFE/THEN THINGS GO TWICE AS WELL."
A STURMLIED
(NAZI BROWNSHIRT ANTHEM)

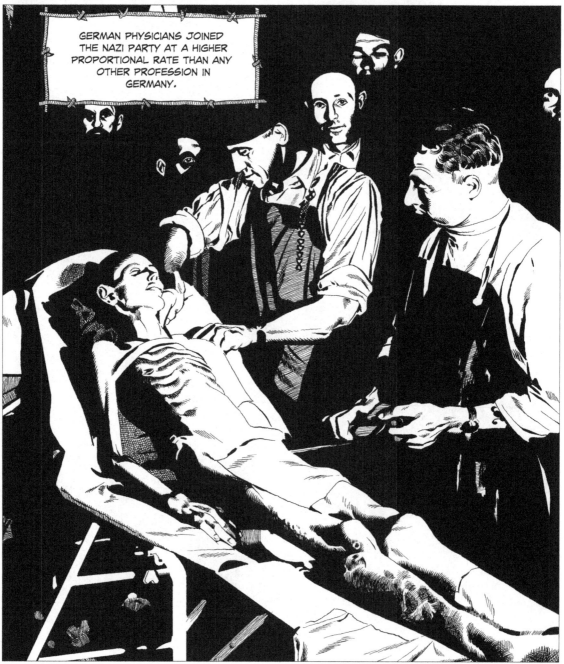

GERMAN PHYSICIANS JOINED THE NAZI PARTY AT A HIGHER PROPORTIONAL RATE THAN ANY OTHER PROFESSION IN GERMANY.

"KRISTER STENDAHL, FORMER DEAN OF THE HARVARD DIVINITY SCHOOL AND THE RETIRED LUTHERAN BISHOP OF STOCKHOLM, TOLD ME THAT WHEN HIS PREDECESSOR, THE SWEDISH BISHOP ERLING EIDEM, WAS ASKED DURING WORLD WAR II TO GO PUBLIC WITH WHAT HE KNEW ABOUT THE DEATH CAMPS, HE REFUSED SAYING THAT AFTER THE WAR, SWEDEN WOULD BE NEEDED AS A MEDIATOR."

JAMES CARROLL
CONSTANTINE'S SWORD

"HAD THE NAZI HIERARCHY ENCOUNTERED UNAMBIGUOUS AND SUSTAINED REVULSION BY NON-JEWISH GERMANS AT THEIR ANTI-SEMITIC POLICIES THERE PROBABLY WOULD HAVE BEEN NO FINAL SOLUTION."

HISTORIAN DEBORAH E. LIPSTADT

HENRY WALLACE, SECRETARY OF COMMERCE UNDER PRESIDENT HARRY TRUMAN WROTE IN HIS DIARY THAT IN 1946 TRUMAN WAS "EXASPERATED" OVER JEWISH PRESSURE THAT HE SUPPORT ZIONIST RULE OVER PALESTINE. WALLACE ADDED, "PRES. TRUMAN EXPRESSED HIMSELF AS BEING VERY MUCH 'PUT OUT' WITH THE JEWS. HE SAID THAT 'JESUS CHRIST COULDN'T PLEASE THEM WHEN HE WAS HERE ON EARTH, SO HOW COULD ANYONE EXPECT THAT I WOULD HAVE ANY LUCK?' PRES. TRUMAN SAID HE HAD NO USE FOR THEM AND DIDN'T CARE WHAT HAPPENED TO THEM."

"HOW CAN WE NOT LAMENT THE LACK OF DISCERNMENT WHICH AT TIMES BECAME EVEN ACQUIESCENCE?"

POPE JOHN-PAUL II

RABBI MARC TANENBAUM, A FOUNDER OF JEWISH-CHRISTIAN DIALOGUE WAS ASKED; "RABBI, TELL ME WHAT MAKES YOU GLAD INSTEAD OF WHAT HURTS YOU." TO WHICH HE REPLIED, "WHAT MAKES US GLAD IS IF YOU DON'T PERSECUTE US ANYMORE."

"PRESSURE ON THE WHITE HOUSE FROM AMERICAN ZIONISTS WAS, AS MR. TRUMAN TOLD ME, SO GREAT THAT: "WELL, THERE'D NEVER BEEN ANYTHING LIKE IT BEFORE, AND THERE WASN'T AFTER. NOT EVEN WHEN I FIRED MACARTHUR, THERE WASN'T. AND I SAID, I ISSUED ORDERS THAT I WASN'T GOING TO SEE ANYONE WHO WAS AN EXTREMIST FOR THE ZIONIST CAUSE, AND I DIDN'T CARE WHO IT WAS."

LATE ON THE MORNING OF MARCH 13 [1948] MR. TRUMAN GOT A TELEPHONE CALL FROM THE STATLER, WHERE HIS OLD FRIEND AND BUSINESS PARTNER EDDIE JACOBSON WAS STAYING. EDDIE WANTED TO COME TO THE WHITE HOUSE TO SEE THE PRESIDENT.

"I SAID TO HIM, 'EDDIE, I'M ALWAYS GLAD TO SEE OLD FRIENDS, BUT THERE'S ONE THING YOU'VE GOT TO PROMISE ME. I DON'T WANT YOU TO SAY A WORD ABOUT WHAT'S GOING ON OVER THERE IN THE MIDDLE EAST. DO YOU PROMISE?' AND HE DID."

A LITTLE LATER EDDIE WAS USHERED INTO THE OVAL ROOM AND THIS IS THE WAY HARRY TRUMAN DESCRIBED WHAT FOLLOWED:

GREAT TEARS WERE RUNNING DOWN HIS CHEEKS, AND I TOOK ONE LOOK AT HIM AND I SAID, "EDDIE, YOU SON OF A BITCH, YOU PROMISED ME YOU WOULDN'T SAY A WORD ABOUT WHAT'S GOING ON OVER THERE." AND HE SAID, "MR. PRESIDENT, I HAVEN'T SAID A WORD, BUT EVERY TIME I THINK OF THE HOMELESS JEWS, HOMELESS FOR THOUSANDS OF YEARS, AND I THINK ABOUT DR. WEIZMANN [CHAIM WEIZMANN, HEAD OF THE WORLD ZIONISTS AND THE FIRST PRESIDENT OF ISRAEL], I START CRYING. I CAN'T HELP IT. HE'S AN OLD MAN, AND HE'S SPENT HIS WHOLE LIFE WORKING FOR A HOMELAND FOR THE JEWS, AND NOW HE'S SICK, AND HE'S IN NEW YORK AND HE WANTS TO SEE YOU. AND EVERY TIME I THINK ABOUT IT I CAN'T HELP CRYING."

CHAIM WEIZMANN

I SAID, "EDDIE, YOU SON OF A BITCH, I OUGHT TO HAVE YOU THROWN RIGHT OUT OF HERE FOR BREAKING YOUR PROMISE; YOU KNEW DAMN GOOD AND WELL I COULDN'T STAND SEEING YOU CRY."

AND HE KIND OF SMILED AT ME, STILL CRYING, THOUGH, AND HE SAID "THANK YOU, MR. PRESIDENT." AND HE LEFT.

AFTER HE WAS GONE, I PICKED UP THE PHONE AND CALLED THE STATE DEPARTMENT, AND I TOLD THEM I WAS GOING TO SEE WEIZMANN. WELL YOU SHOULD HAVE HEARD THE CARRYING-ON. THE FIRST THING THEY SAID – THEY SAID ISRAEL WASN'T EVEN A COUNTRY YET AND DIDN'T HAVE A FLAG OR ANYTHING. THEY SAID IF WEIZMANN COMES TO THE WHITE HOUSE, WHAT ARE WE GOING TO USE FOR A FLAG?

AND I SAID, "LOOK HERE; HE'S STAYING AT THE WALDORF-ASTORIA HOTEL IN NEW YORK, AND EVERY TIME SOME FOREIGN DIGNITARY IS STAYING THERE, THEY PUT SOMETHING OUT. YOU FIND OUT WHAT IT IS, AND WE'LL USE IT. AND I WANT YOU TO CALL ME RIGHT BACK."

ON MARCH 18 CHAIM WEIZMAN CAME TO THE WHITE HOUSE, BUT NO FLAG WAS NECESSARY. HE CAME IN THROUGH THE EAST GATE, AND THE FACT OF HIS VISIT WAS NOT KNOWN UNTIL LATER.

IN ANY CASE, ONLY ELEVEN MINUTES AFTER ISRAEL BECAME A STATE IN MAY, ITS EXISTENCE WAS OFFICIALLY RECOGNIZED BY THE UNITED STATES.

A YEAR LATER, THE CHIEF RABBI OF ISRAEL CAME TO SEE THE PRESIDENT AND HE TOLD HIM, "GOD PUT YOU IN YOUR MOTHER'S WOMB SO THAT YOU COULD BE THE INSTRUMENT TO BRING ABOUT THE REBIRTH OF ISRAEL AFTER TWO THOUSAND YEARS."

AT THAT, GREAT TEARS STARTED ROLLING DOWN HARRY TRUMAN'S CHEEKS."

PLAIN SPEAKING:
AN ORAL BIOGRAPHY OF
HARRY S. TRUMAN
BY MERLE MILLER

"THE WORDS OF THE ANCIENT PSALM RISE FROM OUR HEARTS: *"I HAVE BECOME LIKE A BROKEN VESSEL. I HEAR THE WHISPERING OF MANY – TERROR ON EVERY SIDE – AS THEY SCHEME TOGETHER AGAINST ME; AS THEY PLOT TO TAKE MY LIFE. BUT I TRUST IN YOU, O LORD: I SAY 'YOU ARE MY GOD.'"* (PSALMS 31:13-15). IN THIS PLACE OF MEMORIES, THE MIND AND HEART AND SOUL FEEL IN EXTREME NEED FOR SILENCE.

SILENCE IN WHICH TO REMEMBER. SILENCE IN WHICH TO TRY TO MAKE SOME SENSE OF THE MEMORIES WHICH COME FLOODING BACK. SILENCE BECAUSE THERE ARE NO WORDS STRONG ENOUGH TO DEPLORE THE TERRIBLE TRAGEDY OF THE SHOAH.

MY OWN PERSONAL MEMORIES ARE OF ALL THAT HAPPENED WHEN THE NAZIS OCCUPIED POLAND DURING THE WAR. I REMEMBER MY JEWISH FRIENDS AND NEIGHBORS, SOME OF WHOM PERISHED, WHILE OTHERS SURVIVED. I HAVE COME TO YAD VASHEM TO PAY HOMAGE TO THE MILLIONS OF JEWISH PEOPLE WHO, STRIPPED OF EVERYTHING, ESPECIALLY OF HUMAN DIGNITY WERE MURDERED IN THE HOLOCAUST. MORE THAN HALF A CENTURY HAS PASSED, BUT THE MEMORIES REMAIN.

HERE, AS AT AUSCHWITZ AND MANY OTHER PLACES IN EUROPE, WE ARE OVERCOME BY THE ECHO OF THE HEART-RENDING LAMENTS OF SO MANY. MEN, WOMEN AND CHILDREN, CRY OUT TO US FROM THE DEPTHS OF THE HORROR THAT THEY KNEW. HOW CAN WE FAIL TO HEED THEIR CRY? NO ONE CAN FORGET OR IGNORE WHAT HAPPENED. NO ONE CAN DIMINISH ITS SCALE.

WE WISH TO REMEMBER. BUT WE WISH TO REMEMBER FOR A PURPOSE, NAMELY TO ENSURE THAT NEVER AGAIN WILL EVIL PREVAIL, AS IT DID FOR THE MILLIONS OF INNOCENT VICTIMS OF NAZISM.

HOW COULD MAN HAVE SUCH UTTER CONTEMPT FOR MAN? BECAUSE HE HAD REACHED THE POINT OF CONTEMPT FOR GOD. ONLY A GODLESS IDEOLOGY COULD PLAN AND CARRY OUT THE EXTERMINATION OF A WHOLE PEOPLE.

THE HONOUR GIVEN TO THE *"JUST GENTILES"* BY THE STATE OF ISRAEL AT YAD VASHEM FOR HAVING ACTED HEROICALLY TO SAVE JEWS, SOMETIMES TO THE POINT OF GIVING THEIR OWN LIVES, IS A RECOGNITION THAT NOT EVEN IN THE DARKEST HOUR IS EVERY LIGHT EXTINGUISHED. THAT IS WHY THE PSALMS AND THE ENTIRE BIBLE, THOUGH WELL AWARE OF THE HUMAN CAPACITY FOR EVIL, ALSO PROCLAIMS THAT EVIL WILL NOT HAVE THE LAST WORD.

OUT OF THE DEPTHS OF PAIN AND SORROW, THE BELIEVER'S HEART CRIES OUT: *"I TRUST IN YOU, O LORD: I SAY, YOU ARE MY GOD."* (PSALMS 31:14) JEWS AND CHRISTIANS SHARE AN IMMENSE SPIRITUAL PATRIMONY, FLOWING FROM GOD'S SELF-REVELATION. OUR RELIGIOUS TEACHINGS AND OUR SPIRITUAL EXPERIENCE DEMAND THAT WE OVERCOME EVIL WITH GOOD. WE REMEMBER, BUT NOT WITH ANY DESIRE FOR VENGEANCE OR AS AN INCENTIVE TO HATRED. FOR US, TO REMEMBER IS TO PRAY FOR PEACE AND JUSTICE, AND TO COMMIT OURSELVES TO THEIR CAUSE. ONLY A WORLD AT PEACE, WITH JUSTICE FOR ALL, CAN AVOID REPEATING THE MISTAKES AND TERRIBLE CRIMES OF THE PAST.

AS BISHOP OF ROME AND SUCCESSOR OF THE APOSTLE PETER, I ASSURE THE JEWISH PEOPLE THAT THE CATHOLIC CHURCH, MOTIVATED BY THE GOSPEL LAW OF TRUTH AND LOVE, AND BY NO POLITICAL CONSIDERATIONS, IS DEEPLY SADDENED BY THE HATRED, ACTS OF PERSECUTION AND DISPLAYS OF ANTI-SEMITISM DIRECTED AGAINST THE JEWS BY CHRISTIANS AT ANY TIME AND IN ANY PLACE.

THE CHURCH REJECTS RACISM IN ANY FORM AS A DENIAL OF THE IMAGE OF THE CREATOR IN EVERY HUMAN BEING.

IN THIS PLACE OF SOLEMN REMEMBRANCE, I FERVENTLY PRAY THAT OUR SORROW FOR THE TRAGEDY WHICH THE JEWISH PEOPLE SUFFERED IN THE 20TH CENTURY WILL LEAD TO A NEW RELATIONSHIP BETWEEN CHRISTIANS AND JEWS. LET US BUILD A NEW FUTURE IN WHICH THERE WILL BE NO MORE ANTI-JEWISH FEELING AMONG CHRISTIANS OR ANTI-CHRISTIAN FEELING AMONG JEWS, BUT RATHER THE MUTUAL RESPECT REQUIRED OF THOSE WHO ADORE THE ONE CREATOR AND LORD, AND LOOK TO ABRAHAM AS OUR COMMON FATHER IN FAITH.

THE WORLD MUST HEED THE WARNING THAT COMES TO US FROM THE VICTIMS OF THE HOLOCAUST, AND FROM THE TESTIMONY OF THE SURVIVORS. HERE AT YAD VASHEM THE MEMORY LIVES ON, AND BURNS ITSELF ONTO OUR SOULS. IT MAKES US CRY OUT: *"I HEAR THE WHISPERING OF MANY – TERROR ON EVERY SIDE – BUT I TRUST IN YOU, O LORD: I SAY, 'YOU ARE MY GOD.'"* (PSALMS 31:13-15)

POPE JOHN PAUL II'S SPEECH AT YAD VASHEM IN JERUSALEM 23 MARCH 2000

Acknowledgements & Bibliography

The greatest challenge that I faced in producing this work was in what I had to leave out, so overwhelming is the historical record of Jew Hatred among gentiles.

Richard S. Levy's ANTISEMITISM IN THE MODERN WORLD: An Anthology of Texts (D.C. Heath and Company, Lexington, MA 1991) proved invaluable with the quotes from Voltaire (p.40) Johann Friedrich Benzenberg (p.64), Heinrich von Treitschke (p.72), Gyozo Istoczy (p.100-101), Hermann Bielohlawek (p.117) and Yevgeny Yevseev (p.263). Unfortunately space considerations compelled me to delete the following quote from Edouard Drumont's *Les Juifs contre la France* [The Jews Against France] (Paris, 1899):

"If the circumstances were such that I was invested with an authority which would permit me to save my country, I would turn the leading Jews and their accomplices over to a court martial which would have them shot."

and the following quote from Donald A. Cameron, British Consul-General at Alexandria "a man fully in sympathy with Zionism and much quoted in the Jewish press":

"The Jewish immigrants [into Palestine] will tire of taking in one another's washing at 3 percent, of winning one another's money in the family, and their sons will hasten by train and steamer to win 10 percent in Egypt...The Jew by himself in Palestine will eat his head off; he will kick his stable to pieces."

With Zionist "friends" like this, who needs Zionist enemies? A resource that seemed too good to be true – "1,000 Quotes By and About Jews" at http://www.radioislam.org/quotes/index.htm – turned out to be just that: too good to be true. I went through and read all 1,000 quotes in the course of a couple of afternoons at the library, omitting the most obvious fabrications and redundancies (and overlooking the atrocious spelling and punctuation and egregious number of typos) and restricting myself to those quotes associated with names familiar to the average reader. This process of elimination quickly diminished the list to a couple of dozen potential citations which I forwarded to Lou Copeland for verification or refutation. I was about to begin my portraits of George Washington and Benjamin Franklin when (having detected a distinctly anachronistic flavour to the language and phraseology of both quotes) I chose to do my own research on both gentlemen, finding no reference to anti-Semitic tendencies in the indexes of any of the books available to me.

Sure enough "The Franklin Prophecy", a scathing tirade against the Jews, proved to be a hoax, first published in February, 1934 and still circulating, attributed to the "private diary" of Charles Pinkney, a delegate from South Carolina to the Constitutional Convention. Anti-Semites maintain that the diary is now in the possession of the Franklin Institute in Philadelphia, "a

bald lie which Henry Butler Allen, director of the Institute has often refuted"
(http://www.adl.org/special_reports/franklin_prophecy/print.asp)

The actual quote from George Washington was:

"This tribe of black gentry work more effectually against us than the enemies' arms. They are a hundred times more dangerous to our liberties, and the great cause we are engaged in. It is much to be lamented that each State, long ere this, has not hunted them down as pests to society, and the greatest enemies we have to the happiness of America."

Anti-semites had changed "This tribe of black gentry" – currency speculators who sought to profit by taking advantage of soldiers and others during the Revolutionary War – to "They (the Jews)"

It is worth noting that on a goodwill visit paid to Newport, Rhode Island, during his first term as President, when a goodwill address was presented to him by the Hebrew Congregation of that city, Washington responded by penning "the first presidential declaration of the free and equal status of Jewish-American citizens.":

"For happily, the Government of the United States, which gives to bigotry no sanction, to persecution no assistance, requires only that they who live under its protection should demean themselves as good citizens...May the Children of the Stock of Abraham, who dwell in this land, continue to merit and enjoy the good will of the other Inhabitants; while every one shall sit under his own vine and fig tree, and there shall be none to make him afraid."

I have to admit that I have had no previous experience with just such a research minefield where disinformation abounds in all directions in the interests of making Jew Hatred appear both a) normal and b) endorsed by the giants of our civilization's history. There were a number of judgement calls I was required to make by the nature of the material: as an example, this quote from St. Thomas Aquinas:

"The Jews should not be allowed to keep what they have obtained from others by usury; it were best that they were compelled to work so that they could earn their living instead of doing nothing but becoming more avaricious."

In my view this was more an indictment of usury – the charging of <u>excessive</u> interest on monetary loans – than it was of Jews and consequently didn't qualify as Jew Hatred. Usurious interest is to be deplored wherever – and for whatever ostensible reason – it occurs. The Mark Twain quote that I included falls along the same lines but in my view, the assertion "His success has made the whole human race his enemy" tips the balance in favour of qualifying this as Jew Hatred since it is unlikely that Twain or anyone else would think that a comparable success would make the "whole human race" the enemy of a comparable individual or culture.

I had read the first volume of Holroyd's monumental biography of George Bernard Shaw and had access to the subsequent four. Over two thousand pages there had been no reference to anti-Semitism in any of the four indexes. The entry in "1,000 Quotes By and About Jews" was either a fabrication or a momentary intellectual hiccup.

Of course I found the reference to President Harry Truman by Secretary of Commerce Henry Wallace to be equally suspect, especially in light of the larger extract from Merle Miller's *Plain Speaking,* but decided to make use of it in order to more sharply establish the *volte face* that President Truman experienced from the time of his in-laws' pronounced anti-Semitism towards Eddie Jacobson as documented in *Plain Speaking.* On the other hand, there is the quote from Janey Chiles, a retired Independence, MO schoolteacher referring to Bess Truman's mother, "...Nobody was ever good enough for her, or so it seemed. She was a very, very difficult person, and *there wasn't anybody in town she didn't look down on.*" [emphasis mine] Reportedly she even looked down on Harry Truman after he had become the President of the United States!

I excluded H.G. Wells for his "A careful study of anti-Semitic prejudices and accusations might be of great value to many Jews, who do not adequately realize the irritations they inflict." The "many" to me takes this out of the realm of Jew Hatred. "A careful study of anti-Canadian prejudices and accusations might be of great value to many Canadians." I sure couldn't argue with that. I then re-included him with the quote on page 8 as cited by a letter writer to *The National Post.* A Thomas Jefferson quote proved to be from a letter to President Monroe in 1823 wherein there was no reference to Jews whatsoever. On the website, "Jews" had been substituted for "Europeans". A quote attributed to Franz Liszt – taken from the second edition of his book on the music of Gypsies in Hungary – proved to have been "edited in" by his anti-Semitic Catholic life-partner Carolyn Sayn-Wittgenstein. There's a quote from Robert Louis Stevenson about "Jew storekeepers" who had learned the advantage to be gained from giving farmers unlimited credit, leading the farmers into "irretrievable indebtedness". I think that says more about the folly of using unlimited credit when it is offered than it says about those offering unlimited credit.

Much is made of *President* Ulysses S. Grant expelling the Jews from "The Department" (Tennessee, Mississippi and Kentucky) although he was only a *General* at the time (and the order was "almost immediately rescinded" by President Lincoln).

Regarding Martin Luther's treatise, *On the Jews and Their Lies,* writing in *Lutheran Quarterly* in 1987, Dr. Johannes Wallmann stated, "The assertion that Luther's expressions of anti-Jewish sentiment have been of major and persistent influence in the centuries after the Reformation, and that there exists a continuity between Protestant anti-Judaism and modern, racially oriented anti-Semitism, is at present widespread in the literature; since the Second World War it has understandably become the prevailing opinion." Karl Jaspers wrote, "Da steht das ganze Programm der Nazi Zeit schon." ("There you already have the whole Nazi program"). A sign of just how "madding" this could be, Luther was actually advocating that the Jews be made to live off the soil, unwittingly proposing a return to the condition of the early Middle Ages when the Jews had been in agriculture. Forced off the land, they had gone into commerce and, having been expelled from commerce, into money lending.

In 1994, the Church Council of the Evangelical Lutheran Church in America publicly rejected Luther's anti-Semitic writings, saying: "We who bear his name and heritage must acknowledge with pain the anti-Judaic diatribes contained in Luther's later writings. We reject this violent invective as did many of his companions in the sixteenth century, and we are moved to deep and abiding sorrow at its tragic effects on later generations of Jews. In concert with other Lutherans represented in the Lutheran World Federation, we particularly deplore the appropriation of Luther's words by anti-Semites as part of their teaching of hatred towards the Jews and Judaism in our own day."

In 1995 the Evangelical Lutheran Church in Canada made similar statements and the Austrian Evangelical Church followed suit in 1998. The Austrian Church declared that

"not only individual Christians but also our churches share in the guilt of the Holocaust (Shoah)...we as Protestant Christians are burdened by the late writings of Luther and their demand for expulsion and persecution of the Jews. We reject the contents of these writings."

However, in the same year, The Land Synod of the Lutheran Church of Bavaria issued a declaration saying:

"It is imperative for the Lutheran Church, which knows itself to be indebted to the work and tradition of Martin Luther, to take seriously also his anti-Jewish utterances, to acknowledge their theological function, and to reflect on their consequences."

I still find it hard to believe how much of this material is widely available on the Internet, expecting to be taken at face value and, presumably, finding newer and ever-more-gullible audiences. Henry Ford's *The International Jew* is excerpted throughout "1,000 Quotes By and About Jews". Between 1920 and 1922 he serialized the publication of *The Protocols of the Learned Elders of Zion* in the *Dearborn Independent*, a newspaper he purchased for that express purpose. He not only republished the 1903 hoax (which had already been discredited everywhere in the civilized world), but also included with it numerous articles about Jews in the United States, eventually collecting all the material into the four-volume *The International Jew.*

"Wherever Jewish tendencies are permitted to work unhindered, the result is not 'Americanization', nor 'Anglicization' nor any other distinctive nationalism, but a strong and ruling reversion back to essential 'Judaization'"
                                    Henry Ford,
                                    "Protocols Claim Partial Fulfillment"

Adolf Hitler read the Ford volumes while a prisoner after the failed Beer Hall Putsch in 1923 and credited Ford with his enlightenment on the Jewish problem.

I have here an essay entitled "The Universality of Anti-Semitism" which adopts the mind-boggling posture that there must be a good reason for hating the Jews since hatred of the Jews occurs in all cultures and civilizations! At one point, my Technical Director, Lou Copeland, himself a Jew, said on the phone, "I've read so much of this crap by now, I'm starting to half believe it." It seems to me that that's the core danger.

According to Jonathon Green in *Words Apart: The Language of Prejudice* (Kylie Cathie, London, 1996) there are more insulting terms for blacks and Jews (including those on pages 12 and 18) than for any other racial or cultural groups by a wide margin.

Most of the facts cited in JUDENHASS are taken from THE HOLOCAUST CHRONICLE (Publications International, Ltd., Lincolnwood, Illinois, 2001) the most exhaustive and comprehensive record of the Shoah which I was able to find and which included a year-by-year series of sidebars documenting the descent into the maelstrom. You'll note that my chosen excerpts only go up to the end of 1940, well before the actual beginning of the Shoah, per se. If every school in the English-speaking world owned and taught from THE HOLOCAUST CHRONICLE, I can't imagine that there would be any need for further Holocaust literature.

Unfortunately in this age of diminishing attention spans it seems to me that there is also a need for distillations of the facts that allow even the slowest reader and the most reluctant teacher to comprehend and convey some measure of the enormity of the Shoah and the profound level of enmity against Jews which made it possible. I hope that JUDENHASS – with roughly a 25-minute reading span – will serve that purpose. Out of four years of high school education, it is to be hoped that 25 minutes could be found to teach high school students on the subject...and the on-going significance...of the Holocaust.

The Method & Materials

In my attempted revival of the photorealism drawing style of newspaper strip cartoonists of the 1950s and 60s (foremost among them, Alex Raymond, John Prentice, Stan Drake, Al Williamson and Neal Adams) I needed a great many photographs of the survivors of the Shoah and of the various individuals depicted. Most of these, fortunately, I was able to find on the bookshelves of the Kitchener Public Library. Unfortunately, the quality of my depiction in all cases depended on the clarity of the reproduction I could achieve by photocopying the image, overturning it onto a light table, then tracing every detail in pencil onto tracing paper...then transferring the pencil image by placing the tracing paper image face down on the art board (S-172 Bainbridge Illustration Board) and tracing over it...and then keeping the original photo in close proximity as I tightened the image up in pencil (primarily 3H and

4H Staedtler Mars Lumograph) and then inking it with a Hunt 102 pen nib or a Gillott 290 pen nib. This proved awkward with library books for obvious reasons and I hope all the book-lovers in the audience will forgive me for dismembering my copy of Gerhard Schoenberner's THE YELLOW STAR so that I could have each photo neatly taped next to its pencilled counterpart while I worked to achieve a good likeness. All photographs are deceptive by nature so where I was unable to determine the nature of any given element I tried just to imitate the pattern of light and shadows to the best of my ability.

The Photographs
HC denotes *The Holocaust Chronicle*
YS denotes *The Yellow Star*

Cover – HC p. 584 "These children were among the few who survived imprisonment at Birkenau" UPI/Corbis [uncredited]

Page 1, 4, 5 – YS p.172-173   Panstwowe Muzeum Oswiecim-Brzezinka, Auschwitz [uncredited] plus Contemporary photos [uncredited] Railway Entrance to Auschwitz-Birkenau

---

Page 2 – *The Art of Will Eisner* Cat Yronwode (Kitchen Sink Press, Princeton, Wisconsin 1982): Will Eisner (p.19); "Of Supermen and Kids with Dreams" by Thomas Andrae, *Overstreet Comic Book Price Guide* (Overstreet Publications, Cleveland TN, 1988): Jerry Siegel and Joe Shuster (p.A-93); *The Comic Book Makers* Joe Simon with Jim Simon (Crestwood/II Publications, New York, 1990): Joe Simon (p.26), Jack Kirby (p.85); "How the Jews Created the Comic-Book Industry" by Arie Kaplan *Comic Book Marketplace* No.116 October 2004 (Gemstone Publishing, Missouri) (originally published in *Reform Judaism* magazine): Max Gaines (p.26) Stan Lee (p.36) Bob Kane (p.38); *Alter Ego* No.44 January, 2005 (TwoMorrows Publishing, Raleigh, NC): Sheldon Mayer (p.5). [photos uncredited]

Page 3 – YS p. 249 "Liberated prisoners in Buchenwald" Imperial War Museum (IWM), London (uncredited)

Pages 6-7 – "Arbeit Macht Frei" road entrance to Auschwitz Birkenau. Although usually translated as "Work Will Make You Free" or "Work Makes Freedom" my German-English dictionary translates "Macht" as "Power" so the notorious slogan is actually three nouns: Work, Power, Freedom

---

Pages 8-10 – "Bodies removed by German civilians at Gusen" Mauthausen; Yad Veshem Photo Archive

---

Pages 11-14 – "Close-up of corpses piled in the crematorium mortuary in the newly liberated Dachau concentration camp, Dachau, Germany, May, 1945" Yad Vashem Photo Archive

---

Pages 15, 16 – HC p. 451 – "Although *Sonderkommandos* assisted the Nazis in order to spare their own lives (at least temporarily), they were often hated by those Jews doomed to die." Bilderdienst Süddeutscher Verlag [uncredited]

Page 17 – "A survivor stokes smoldering human remains in a crematorium oven that is still lit. Dachau, Germany April 29-May 1, 1945" Yad VashemPhoto Archive

---

Pages 18, 19, 20 – HC p. 593 – "The man closest to the camera, a Hungarian Jew, was so thin that one can see his spine from above. Victims of such severe cases of starvation and malnutrition had little chance of survival." Archive Photos [uncredited]

Pages 21, 22 – "Dachau After Liberation" LIBERATION PHOTOGRAPHS Yad Vashem Photo Archive

---

Page 23 – YS p. 22 "Nationwide Pogrom; burning synagogue, Euskirchen" Stadtarchiv Euskirchen [Sammlung Otto Mertens]

Page 24 [inset figure] – YS p.197 "Muselman" "As a prisoner neared death from starvation, camp jargon nicknamed him 'Muselman'" The Imperial War Museum (IWM), London [uncredited]

Page 25 – Martin Luther – dust jacket illustration *Luther A Biography* which has POOF disappeared from the Kitchener Public Library system. I can only hope that it has gone to a far, far better place.

Page 26 – Voltaire at age forty, after a pastel portrait by Quentin de la Tour (Arch. Phot. Paris), modified in light of Jean Huber's sketches (Roger-Viollet)

Page 30 – Mark Twain – *Mark Twain A to Z* R. Kent Rasmussen (Facts on File, Inc., New York, 1995) cover photo c. 1906-1910 [no attribution]; H.L. Mencken *H.L. Mencken* Vincent Fitzpatrick (Mercer University Press, Macon, GA, 2004) dust jacket photo [no attribution]

Page 32-33 – This image of Adolf Hitler appeared twice in *The National Post* during 2006-07 with no studio or photographer credit

Page 34 – Hermann Göring – "At the reception for Göring's second wedding" *World War II Vol.3* (Time-Life Books, Alexandria, VA, 1977) p. 80-81, Heinrich Hoffmann

Page 35 – Harry S. Truman – "Reluctant candidate...1944 Democratic National Convention" p.96 *St. Louis Post-Dispatch* [uncredited] *Truman: A Centenary Remembrance* Robert H. Ferrell (The VikingPress, New York, 1984)]

Page 36 – Pope Pius XI – *The Vatican in the Age of the Dictators 1922-1945* Anthony Richard Ewart Rhodes (Holt Rhinehart Winston, 1973) p. 192 Radio Times Holton Picture Library [uncredited]

Page 37 – Neville Chamberlain – "Peace in our time" announcement Central Press/Getty Images [uncredited]; Laura "Aunt Polly" Delano – *The Roosevelts of Hyde Park: An Untold Story* Elliott Roosevelt and James Brough (G.P. Putnam's Sons, New York, 1973) [photo uncredited]

Pages 36-41 [background] 43 [upper left] – "Ecce Homo 1945" [Latin: Behold, The Man] refers to Pilate's declaration in presenting the scourged Jesus to the Jewish Elders in John 19:5 Imperial War Museum (IWM) London (uncredited)

Page 38 – T. S. Eliot *Eliot's New Life* Lyndall Gordon (Oxford University Press, 1988) jacket photograph by Man Ray

Page 39 – Heinrich Himmler *World War II* Jon Sutherland & Diane Canwell (Prospero Books, London, 2003) p. 228 (uncredited)

Page 40 – YS p. 248 "Liberated prisoner in Dachau 29 April 45" The Imperial War Museum (IWM) London [uncredited]

Page 40 [inset panel] – YS p.238 "Auschwitz, January 27, 1945" Panstwowe Muzeum Oswiecim-Brzezinka, Auschwitz [uncredited]

Page 41 – HC p. 601 "This survivor of Bergen-Belsen was found in agony at liberation. Internment in Hitler's camps had long-term – often calamitous – psychological and physical effects upon survivors" Yad Vashem Photo Archives [uncredited]

Page 40-41 – Crematorium IV at Auschwitz-Birkenau HC p. 339 ("under construction") p. 407 ("could burn almost 1500 bodies a day") Yad Vashem Photo Archives [uncredited]

Page 42 – Toronto Public Library Photo Archive "Holocaust" [no attribution]

Page 43 – Pope John Paul II - *Pope John Paul II A Tribute* (Time Inc. Home Entertainment, 1999) p. 103 Franco Origlia/SYGMA

Page 44-45 – South Portico of the White House – *SOUTH PORTICO/1948: Truman: A Centenary Remembrance* Robert H. Ferrell (The Viking Press, New York, 1984) p. 157 – United Press International [uncredited] *SOUTH LAWN FOLIAGE/1948: Mr. President* by William Hillman (Farrar, Straus and Young, New York, 1952) photo by Alfred Wagg; *SOUTH PORTICO: An Invitation to the White House* Hillary Rodham Clinton (Simon & Schuster New York, 2000) p. 150-151 Robert Clark, p. 154 Sharon Farmer/White House Photo Office; *DETAIL MAIN FLOOR SOUTH PORTICO:* (ibid) p. 135 Todd Eberle (used *without* the permission of the William J. Clinton Presidential Commission); *IONIC CAPITALS ON COLUMNS OF THE NORTH PORTICO: Our Changing White House* edited by Wendell Garrett (Northeastern University Press, 1995) p. 43 Richard Cheek; *FIRST FLOOR WINDOWS/SOUTH PORTICO:* (ibid) p.49 Jack Boucher, *Historic American Buildings Survey BALUSTRADE AND SOUTHEAST CORNER:* (ibid) p.51 Jack Boucher, *Historic American Buildings Survey*

I have chosen to depict the second floor "Truman Balcony" which was slated for construction "early in 1948" according to *Truman: A Centenary Remembrance* on the assumption that construction had been completed by March of 1948 (or at least "only eleven minutes after Israel became a state in May" of that year) (or, at least by "a year later" at the time of the Chief Rabbi's visit). I have depicted the plain white railings which were originally installed (I suspect to "keep a lid" on costs which were "around $10,000" and which had consequently aroused public and Congressional ire). These simple railings were replaced at a later date by more ornate railings matching those of the lower floor on the South Portico commensurate with the White House's Georgian Revival architectural motif.

Page 44 – (inset top) see *"attribution Page 35"* (inset middle) "At work in the Senate Office Building, 1940" *Truman: A Centenary Remembrance* Robert H. Farrell (The Viking Press, New York, 1984) p.87 HS Truman Library [uncredited]

Page 45 – (inset middle and bottom) *Truman: A Centenary Remembrance* Robert H. Farrell (The Viking Press, New York, 1984) dust jacket photo © 1983 Associated Press [uncredited]

Pages 46-47 – Pope John Paul II at the Wailing Wall, Jerusalem, March, 2000 "where he follows the tradition of placing a prayer request in one of the cracks of the ancient fortress wall." *John Paul II* Enquirer Special Vol.VII No.1 (American Media, Inc. Boca Raton, FL, 2002) p.96 [no attribution]

Page 49 – Harry S. Truman – "Friday April 13, 1945...the new President..." *Truman: A Centenary Remembrance* Robert H. Farrell (The Viking Press, New York, 1984) p. 111 United Press International [uncredited]; Pope John Paul II - "The Pope incenses the altar at Sun Devil Stadium in Tempe, Arizona, during his 1987 visit to the United States" *John Paul II: A Light for the World,* Sister Mary Ann Walsh, editor (Sheed & Ward, Lanham, MD) p.57 Arturo Mari (?) *L'Osservatore Romano* (Vatican newspaper)

Special Thanks to Caroline Waddell
United States Holocaust Memorial Museum
for providing the following photographs:

Pages 24-27 USHMM 04508, Pages 28-31 USHMM 28276,
Pages 34-35 [background] USHMM 11127, Page 48 – USHMM 80118

Special Thanks as well to Pauline Testerman
of the Harry S. Truman Presidential Library
for providing the following photographs:

Page 44 (bottom inset) Eddie Jacobson
© Internat'l New Photo (now UPI)
photo by Arthur E. Scott
HST 77-891
Page 45 (top inset) Chaim Weizmann
© Brown-Suarez Photo, Washington DC
photo uncredited
HST 59-848

59494625R00037

Made in the USA
Columbia, SC
04 June 2019